ISBN 978-0-266-26191-9
PIBN 10906905

English
Français
Deutsche
Italiano
Español
Português

www.forgottenbooks.com

Mythology Photography **Fiction**
Fishing Christianity **Art** Cooking
Essays Buddhism Freemasonry
Medicine **Biology** Music **Ancient
Egypt** Evolution Carpentry Physics
Dance Geology **Mathematics** Fitness
Shakespeare **Folklore** Yoga Marketing
Confidence Immortality Biographies
Poetry **Psychology** Witchcraft
Electronics Chemistry History **Law**
Accounting **Philosophy** Anthropology
Alchemy Drama Quantum Mechanics
Atheism Sexual Health **Ancient History**
Entrepreneurship Languages Sport
Paleontology Needlework Islam
Metaphysics Investment Archaeology
Parenting Statistics Criminology
Motivational

AT THE AMERICAN ART GALLERIES

MADISON SQUARE SOUTH, NEW YORK

BEGINNING WEDNESDAY, JANUARY 4TH, 1922

AND CONTINUING UNTIL THE DATE OF SALE

———

VALUABLE PEARLS
DIAMOND AND OTHER JEWELRY
CABINET GEMS

FINE OLD LACES

AND

EXPENSIVE FUR GARMENTS

————

TO BE SOLD AT UNRESTRICTED PUBLIC SALE

BY ORDER OF EXECUTORS

AT THE AMERICAN ART GALLERIES

ON THURSDAY AFTERNOON, JANUARY 12TH

BEGINNING AT 2.15 O'CLOCK

No. 225—Hudson Bay Sable Coat

ILLUSTRATED CATALOGUE

OF

VALUABLE PEARLS
DIAMOND AND OTHER JEWELRY
CABINET GEMS

FINE OLD LACES

AND

EXPENSIVE FUR GARMENTS

TO BE SOLD AT UNRESTRICTED PUBLIC SALE

BY ORDER OF EXECUTORS, TO CLOSE AN ESTATE

AT THE AMERICAN ART GALLERIES
MÄDISON SQUARE SOUTH, NEW YORK

ON THURSDAY AFTERNOON, JANUARY 12TH, 1922

THE SALE WILL BE CONDUCTED BY

MR. THOMAS E. KIRBY
AND HIS ASSISTANTS, MR. OTTO BERNET AND MR. H. H. PARKE, OF THE

AMERICAN ART ASSOCIATION, MANAGERS
MADISON SQUARE SOUTH, NEW YORK
1922

THE AMERICAN ART ASSOCIATION
DESIGNS ITS CATALOGUES AND DIRECTS
ALL DETAILS OF ILLUSTRATION
TEXT AND TYPOGRAPHY

CONDITIONS OF SALE

I.   **Rejection of bids:** Any bid which is not commensurate with the value of the article offered or which is merely a nominal or fractional advance may be rejected by the auctioneer if in his judgment such bid would be likely to affect the sale injuriously.

II.   **The buyer:** The highest bidder shall be the buyer, and if any dispute arises between two or more bidders, the auctioneer shall either decide the same or put up for re-sale the lot so in dispute.

III.   **Identification and part payment by buyer:** The name of the buyer of each lot shall be given immediately on the sale thereof, and when so required, each buyer shall sign a card giving the lot number, amount for which sold, and his or her name and address.

Payment at the actual time of the sale shall be made of all or such part of the purchase prices as may be required.

If the two foregoing conditions are not complied with, the lot or lots so purchased may at the option of the auctioneer be put up again and re-sold.

IV.   **Risk after purchase:** Title passes upon the fall of the auctioneer's hammer and thereafter neither the consignor nor the Association is responsible for the loss or any damage to any article occasioned by theft, fire, breakage or any other cause.

V.   **Delivery of purchases:** Delivery of *any* purchases will be made only upon payment of the total amount due for *all* purchases at the sale.

Deliveries will be made at the place of sale or at the storage warehouse to which purchases may have been removed.

Deliveries at the American Art Galleries will be made only between the hours of 9 A. M. and 1 P. M. on sales' days and on other days—except holidays, when no deliveries will be made— between the hours of 9 A. M. and 5 P. M.

Deliveries at places of sale other than the American Art Galleries will be made only during the forenoon following the day of sale unless by special notice or arrangement to the contrary.

Deliveries at the storage warehouse to which goods may have been sent will be made on any day other than holidays between the hours of 9 and 5.

Deliveries of any purchases of small articles likely to be lost or mislaid may be made at the discretion of the auctioneer during the session of the sale at which they were sold.

VI. **Storage in default of prompt payment and calling** for goods: Articles not paid for in full and either not called for by the purchaser or delivered upon his or her order by noon of the day following that of the sale will be turned over by the Association to some carter to be carried to and stored in some warehouse until the time of the delivery therefrom to the purchaser, and the cost of such cartage and storage will be charged against the purchaser and the risk of loss or damage occasioned by such removal or storage will be upon the purchaser.

> NOTE: The Limited space of the Delivery Rooms of the Association makes the above requirements necessary, and it is not alone for the benefit of the Association, but also for that of its patrons, whose goods otherwise would have to be so crowded as to be subject to damage and loss.

VII. **Shipping:** Shipping, boxing or wrapping of purchases is a business in which the Association is in no wise engaged, and will not be performed by the Association for purchasers. The Association will, however, afford to purchasers every facility for employing at current and reasonable rates carriers and packers; doing so, however, without any assumption of responsibility on its part for the acts and charges of the parties engaged for such service.

VIII: **Guaranty:** The Association exercises great care to catalogue every lot correctly and endeavors therein and also at the actual time of sale to point out any error, defect or imperfection, but guaranty is not made either by the owner or the Association of the correctness of the description, genuineness, authenticity or condition of any lot and no sale will be set aside on account of any incorrectness, error of cataloguing or imperfection not noted or pointed out. Every lot is sold "as is" and without recourse.

Every lot is on public exhibition one or more days prior to its sale, and the Association will give consideration to the opinion of any trustworthy expert to the effect that any lot has been incorrectly catalogued and in its judgment may thereafter sell the lot as catalogued or make mention of the opinion of such expert, who thereby will become responsible for such damage as might result were his opinion without foundation.

IX. **Buying on order:** Buying or bidding by the Association for responsible parties on orders transmitted to it by mail, telegraph or telephone will be faithfully attended to without charge or commission. Any purchases so made will be subject to the foregoing conditions of sale *except* that, in the event of a purchase of a lot of one or more books by or for a purchaser who has not through himself or his agent been present at the exhibition or sale, the Association will permit such lot to be returned within ten days from the date of sale and the purchase money will be refunded if the lot in any manner differs from its catalogue description.

Orders for execution by the Association should be written and given with such plainness as to leave no room for misunderstanding. Not only should the lot number be given, but also the title, and bids should be stated to be so much for the lot, and when the lot consists of one or more volumes of books or objects of art, the bid per volume or piece should also be stated. If the one transmitting the order is unknown to the Association, a deposit should be sent or reference submitted. Shipping directions should also be given.

Priced Catalogues: Priced copies of the catalogue or any session thereof, will be furnished by the Association at charges commensurate with the duties involved in copying the necessary information from the records of the Association.

AMERICAN ART ASSOCIATION,

American Art Galleries,

Madison Square South,

New York City.

CATALOGUE

AFTERNOON SALE

THURSDAY, JANUARY 12, 1922

AT THE AMERICAN ART GALLERIES

BEGINNING AT 2.15 O'CLOCK

Catalogue Numbers 1 to 217, Inclusive

1—FIVE SMALL COLLARS
Point de Paris.

Length, 12 inches to 14 inches.

2—COLLAR AND CUFFS
Embroidered filet.

Length, 30 inches; width, 6 inches.

Cuffs: Length, 9 inches; width, 3 inches.

3—COLLAR
Brussels pillow lace. Lily pattern.

Length, 1 yard 10 inches; width, 5 inches.

4—THREE SMALL COLLARS AND ONE PAIR OF CUFFS
Valenciennes and Brussels pillow lace. Modern.

Length, 14 inches.

5—COLLAR

Brussels pillow lace. Scroll pattern.

Length, 42 inches; width, 6 inches.

6—COLLAR

Brussels lace. Modern.

Neckband, 15 inches; width, 7 inches.

7—COLLAR

Modern Bruges Roselline pillow lace.

Length, 34 inches; width, 3½ inches.

8—COLLAR AND CUFFS

Embroidered filet.

Length, 28 inches; width, 6 inches.

9—TWO LACE COLLARS

Embroidered net.

Length, 14 inches; width, 3½ inches.

10—NEEDLEPOINT COLLAR AND CUFFS

Cuffs, sixteenth century pattern.

Collar: Length, 13 inches; width, 1½ inches.

Cuffs: Length, 9 inches; width, 4¼ inches.

11—COLLAR AND YOKE OF VENETIAN NEEDLEPOINT

Modern.

Neckband, 16 inches.

12—TWO HONITON LACE COLLARS AND TWO STRIPS MODERN BRUSSELS LACE

Collars, English, middle of the nineteenth century.

Collars: 14 inches.

Lace: Each piece, 20 inches.

13—COLLAR AND CUFFS

Brussels pillow-made lace. Modern.

Collar: Length, 32 inches; width, 5 inches.

Cuffs: Length, 9 inches; width, 4 inches.

14—Lace Cuffs
Pillow-made. Reticello pattern. Modern.

Length, 9 inches; width, 5 inches.

15—Collars and Cuffs
Modern Venetian Point.

Large Collar: 8 inches deep.
Small Collar: Length, 14 inches; width, 2¼ inches.
Cuffs: Length, 12 inches; width, 4 inches.

16—One Small Collar Brussels Needlepoint and One Lot Short-lengths Narrow Lace

Collar: Length, 15½ inches.

17—Two Large Collars in Black Silk Guipure

(a) Length, 2 yards by 12 inches.
(b) Length, 1 yard 15 inches by 7 inches.

18—Two Bands of Applied Lace and One Strip of Lille Lace

Longest piece, 29 inches; width, 4½ inches.

19—Collar and Lace to Match
Modern Brussels.

Longest piece, 1 yard 8 inches.

20—Three Lace Handkerchiefs

15 inches square.

21—Pair of Black Chantilly Lace Sleeve Ruffles and One Lot of Short-lengths Chantilly Edging

Longest piece, 2 yards 13 inches; width, 2 inches.

22—Lace Yoke
Modern Brussels.

Width, 17 inches.

23—Border and Two Sleeves of Valenciennes Lace
Border, leaf and berry pattern, "wire" ground.

Length, 3 yards.

Sleeves, different pattern.

Length, 13 inches.

24—THREE SMALL VEILS

Black Brussels net and Chantilly. About 1870.

> *Lengths, 19 inches, 30 inches and 2 yards, 14 inches.*
> *Widths, 8 inches and 13 inches.*

25—VEIL

Black Brussels net trimmed with Chantilly. About 1870.

> *Length, 1 yard; width, 18 inches.*

26—SQUARE VEIL OF BLACK SPANISH LACE

About 1830.

> *1 yard 16 inches square.*

27—LACE PIN-CUSHION COVER AND TWO LACE TABS

Fine examples of pillow lace, made by Miss N. F.

> *Cover: Diameter, 9½ inches; tabs, 2½ inches by 7 inches.*

28—BARBE OF FINE BRUSSELS PILLOW LACE

Unusual dolphin pattern. About 1870.

> *Length, 1 yard 13 inches; width, 6½ inches.*

29—TWO BARBES OF VALENCIENNES LACE

Sprig pattern on "wire" ground.

> *Length, 1 yard 28 inches; width, 6 inches.*

30—CHANTILLY BARBE

Fine quality. Rose and sprig pattern. Bought in Paris, 1874.

> *Length, 1 yard 16 inches; width, 11 inches*

31—TWO PAIRS OF LACE MITTS

Black and white. Middle of the nineteenth century.

> *Length, 12 inches.*

32—SMALL FICHU

Black Spanish lace, machine-made, pattern outlined by hand. Peony design.

> *Length, 1 yard 32 inches; width, 29 inches.*

33—FICHU

Black Spanish lace, pillow-made.

Length, 2 yards 6 inches; width, 31 inches.

34—BLACK SPANISH LACE FICHU

Length, 2 yards 14 inches.

35—SCARF

Black Spanish lace, pillow-made. Rose pattern.

Length, 2 yards 18 inches; width, 9 inches.

36—INFANT'S LACE CAP AND EMBROIDERED BIB

37—PARASOL COVER OF SPANISH LACE

Diameter, 36 inches.

38—LACE PARASOL COVER

Fine black Chantilly. Floral pattern with trellis band.

Diameter, 16 inches.

39—BRUSSELS LACE PARASOL COVER

Scroll and floral pattern.

Diameter, 34 inches.

40—PARASOL COVER

Tatting.

Diameter, 29 inches.

41—COVER AND SMALL DOILY OF MEXICAN DRAWNWORK

Cover, 12 inches by 20 inches.

Doily, 6 inches square.

42—TWO LACE-TRIMMED DOILIES

Point de Paris. Bird design.

Diameter, 7 inches.

43—VALENCIENNES LACE AND LACE-EDGED EMBROIDERED BANDS

Twelve lengths.

Longest piece, 2 yards; width 1¾ inches.

44—Border of Fine Valenciennes Lace

Carnation pattern. Three lengths.

Length, 14 yards; width, 7 inches.

45—Four Strips Valenciennes Edging

Longest piece, 3 yards; width, 1¼ inches.

46—Border and Insertion of Fine Valenciennes Lace

Rose pattern. Two lengths.

Lengths, 2 yards 21 inches and 11 inches; width, 4 inches.

Insertion (scroll pattern): Length, 1 yard 32 inches; width, 1½ inches.

47—Mechlin Lace

Sprig pattern. Two lengths.

Lengths: 33 inches and 1 yard 35 inches.

Widths: 2½ and 1½ inches.

48—Mechlin Lace

Sprig pattern, scalloped edge. Three lengths.

Lengths, 34 inches and 26 inches; width, 2½ inches.

49—One Lot of Fine Mechlin Lace

(A) Straight edge with dots.

Length, 24 inches; width, 4¼ inches.

(B) Three lengths sprig and dot pattern.

Longest piece: Length, 27½ inches; width, 3½ inches.

50—Strip of Fine Mechlin

Flower and sprig pattern.

Length, 2 yards 22 inches; width, 3½ inches.

51—Four Strips of Mechlin Lace

Leaf and sprig pattern.

Longest piece, 1 yard 23 inches; width, 4 inches.

52—Mechlin Lace

Flower and bud pattern.

Length, 3 yards 32 inches; width, 4½ inches.

53—ONE LOT OF NARROW BRUSSELS NEEDLEPOINT

Longest piece, 26 inches.

54—BRUSSELS PILLOW LACE

Ribbon and lily pattern. Four lengths.

Length, 3 yards; width, 3½ inches.

55—BRUSSELS LACE

Medallion pattern.

Length, 3 yards 29 inches; width, 3 inches.

56—STRIP OF BRUSSELS APPLIQUÉ

Fine quality. Ribbon and basket pattern.

Length, 4 yards; width, 8½ inches.

57—BRUSSELS APPLIQUÉ

Three lengths.

Length, 3 yards 27 inches; width, 5 inches.

58—STRIP OF BRUSSELS LACE

Scroll and flower pattern.

Length, 1 yard 5 inches; width, 5 inches.

59—BORDER OF FINE BRUSSELS POINT AND PILLOW LACE

Scroll and leaf pattern.

Two lengths, each 1 yard 9 inches; width, 4 inches.

60—TWO STRIPS OF MODERN BRUSSELS LACE

Lengths, 1 yard 9 inches and 1 yard 16 inches; width, 4 inches.

61—BAND OF BRUGES PILLOW LACE

"Pot" lace. Modern.

Length, 5 yards; width, 3 inches.

62—BRUGES PILLOW LACE

Scroll and flower pattern.

Length, 3 yards 27 inches; width, 4½ inches.

63—STRIP OF POINT D'ANGLETERRE

With details in *fond de neige*. Eighteenth century.

Length, 1 yard 23 inches; width, 2¾ inches.

64—STRIP OF POINT D'ANGLETERRE

Candelabra pattern. Flemish, early eighteenth century. Two lengths.

Lengths, 1 yard 17 inches, 14½ inches; width, 3¼ inches.

65—STRIP OF POINT D'ANGLETERRE LACE

Ribbon motif with details in *fond de neige*. Three lengths. Flemish, eighteenth century.

Lengths, 23 inches, 23 inches and 16 inches; width, 3½ inches.

66—STRIP OF NEEDLEPOINT AND PILLOW LACE

Italian, Burano. Bought in 1904.

Length, 5 yards 24 inches; width, 7½ inches.

67—STRIP OF NEEDLEPOINT AND PILLOW LACE

Same as the preceding.

Length, 3 yards 10 inches; width, 5¾ inches.

68—MALTESE WHITE SILK LACE

Three lengths.

Length, 7 yards; width, 2½ inches.

69—TWO STRIPS OF MALTESE SILK LACE

Length, 5 yards 11 inches; width, 1½ inches.

Length, 3 yards 23 inches; width, 5 inches.

70—TWO SQUARES SWISS EMBROIDERY

6 inches square.

71—BAND OF HARDANGER CUTWORK

Modern.

Length, 1 yard 21 inches; width, 3¼ inches.

72—FIVE STRIPS OF POINT APPLIQUÉ

Flower pattern.

Longest piece, 1 yard 3 inches; width, 9 inches.

73—VENETIAN LACE, PILLOW AND NEEDLEPOINT

Modern. Foliated scroll pattern. Three lengths.

Longest piece, 31 inches; width, 4 inches.

74—VENETIAN NEEDLEPOINT LACE

Scroll pattern. Two bands and four pieces to match.

*Bands, lengths 21 and 22 inches; width, 3½ inches.
(4) 8 and 10 inches by 6 inches.*

75—FILET INSERTION

Two lengths.

Lengths, 2 yards 5 inches and 1 yard 21 inches; widths 2¼ and 2½ inches.

76—FILET EDGING AND INSERTION

Three lengths.

Lengths, 2 yards 14 inches, 2 yards 25 inches and 1 yard 7 inches.

Widths, 2 inches, 2 inches and ½ inch.

77—FILET EDGING

Different patterns.

Lengths, 4 and 2 yards; width, 1 inch.

78—SPANISH BLOND LACE

Five lengths.

Lengths, 1 yard and 22 inches; width, 3 inches.

79—SPANISH BLOND LACE

Length, 5 yards 13 inches; width, 4 inches.

80—BLACK CHANTILLY LACE CAP

About 1830.

Length, 1 yard 10 inches; width, 11 inches.

81—BLACK CLUNY LACE INSERTION

Leaf and scroll pattern.

Length, 2 yards 25 inches; width, 2¼ inches.

82—BLACK SILK LACE

Guipure. Scroll pattern.

Length, 7 yards; width, 6½ inches.

83—BLACK CHANTILLY INSERTION

Ten lengths.

Length, 6 yards 22 inches; width, 1½ inches.

84—BLACK CHANTILLY LACE INSERTION
Flower and lattice pattern.   Five lengths.

Length, 15 yards 11 inches; width, ½ inch.

85—BLACK CHANTILLY LACE INSERTION
Vine pattern.   Two lengths.

Length, 7 yards; width, 3 inches.

86—BLACK CHANTILLY LACE INSERTION
Vine pattern.   Five lengths.

Length, 5 yards 10 inches; width, 1¾ inches.

87—ONE LOT OF BLACK CHANTILLY LACE EDGING
Maple-leaf pattern.   Odd lengths.

20 yards.   Longest piece, 2 yards 18 inches; width, 1¼ inches.

88—ONE LOT OF BLACK CHANTILLY LACE EDGING
Leaf pattern.   Odd lengths.

20 yards.   Longest piece, 9 yards 3 inches; widths, 1¼ to 3½ inches.

89—BLACK CHANTILLY LACE
Pointed-leaf pattern.   Three lengths.

Longest piece, 5 yards 26 inches; width, 4¾ inches.

90—BLACK LACE EDGING
Cluny.

Length, 31 yards; width, ½ inch.

91—CLUNY LACE
Black and white.

Length, 3 yards 15 inches; width, 5 inches.

92—BLACK SILK SPANISH LACE
Floral pattern.   Nine lengths.

Longest piece, 1 yard 24 inches; width, 4 inches.

93—BLACK CHANTILLY LACE SHAWL
Hand-made.   Floral pattern with lattice border.

Length, 3 yards; width, 1 yard 18 inches.

94—Bolero Jacket

Black Chantilly lace.

Depth, 14 inches.

95—Deep Cape of Renaissance Silk Braid Lace

Neckband, 18 inches; depth, 13½ inches.

96—Bridal Point Appliqué Lace

Dress pattern: Skirt, bodice and sleeves. Six pieces.

Skirt: Length, 39 to 55 inches; width, 4 yards.

97—Two Japanese Embroidered and Painted Silk Fan-Mounts

Of white silk, embroidered in colored silks and painted in gold and colors, one with sprays of Flowers and Leaves, one with flying Cranes and Water plants.

Lengths, 9½ and 8½ inches.

98—Two French Fans *Eighteenth Century*

One with pierced, carved, painted and inlaid ivory guards and mother-of-pearl sticks. One with pierced, carved and painted ivory guards and sticks. Painted silk and paper mounts.

Lengths, 10¾ and 9 inches.

99—Two Fans

One with tortoise-shell guards (having applied carved monogram and crest) and blades, one with mother-of-pearl guards (one broken). Both with silk mounts painted, one with oval miniature and birds, one with Venus in car and Amorino.

Lengths, 12 and 11½ inches.

100—American Fan

Yellow carved and painted tortoise-shell guard and blades; mount of painted and spangled cambric with insertions of swallows in painted and spangled net.

Length, 9½ inches.

101—FRENCH FAN *Eighteenth Century*

Pierced, carved and painted ivory guards and blades, mount of paper painted, on one side with Watteau figure subject, and on the other with view of Church in landscape.

Length, 10¾ *inches.*

102—ONE SPANISH AND ONE FRENCH FAN

One with mother-of-pearl guards (one broken) and blades, and silk mount painted with "Bull-fight"; one with tortoise-shell and ostrich-feather guards and blades.

Lengths, 18 *and* 14½ *inches.*

103—TWO FRENCH FANS *Eighteenth Century*

One with carved and painted ivory guards, pierced ivory blades and plain mount of later date; one with mother-of-pearl guards and blades, carved and lacquered, and with white silk mount painted with figures and scrolls.

Lengths, 10 *and* 7½ *inches.*

104—SIX FANS

Four of sandal-wood with pierced blades; one with mount of black silk embroidered in colors, pierced composition blades and carved ebonized wood guards.

Lengths, 13¾ *and* 10½ *inches.*

105—FRENCH PARASOL HANDLE AND FINIAL

Tortoise-shell. Handle carved with knots and spiral flutings.

Length, 11½ *inches.*

VALUABLE PEARLS, DIAMONDS, GOLD AND OTHER JEWELRY AND ARTISTIC GEMS

106—TWO REPOUSSÉ CHAMBER CANDLESTICKS

Nuremberg, Circa 1799

Short balustered bobêche, with large bossed and scrolled vine enrichment. Long flange handle adorned with paneled figures and mask terminal. One rim near handle defective.

107—JEWELED TURQUOISE SILVER BELT

Syrian Eighteenth Century

Flexible silver band of three flat strands; hinged for clasp and at intervals. Enriched with gold filigree plaquettes adorned with small uncut turquoises.

. Length, 26¾ inches.

108—JEWELED CORAL SILVER GIRDLE

Syrian Eighteenth Century

Composed of three bossed filigree linked balls, a band of three flexible strands, bossed with coral and a plaited strand at other end, terminated with a loop and hook, turquoise enriched bosses.

Length, 35½ inches.

109—TWO STRANDS OF CORAL BEADS

(A) Finely matched graduated round pink beads.

(B) Tubular beads of rich rose-red.

Lengths, 21 and 15 inches.

110—CORAL BEAD NECKLACE

Rich pink round beads, with two frontal strands and single at back.

Length, 27 inches.

111—TWO STRANDS OF CORAL BEADS

Rich deep round beads; finely graduated.

Length, 18½ inches.

112—FOUR CONNECTED STRANDS OF CORAL BEADS

Deep coral; finely matched and graduated.

Length, 21 inches.

113—MOONSTONE AND CRYSTAL NECKLACE

Graduated round beads, with faceted stops of crystal. Silver snap.

Length, 16 inches.

114—TWO GOLD MOUNTED ABALONE PEARL NECKLACES

(A) Oval purple and green abalones, with gold rims and circular clasps.

(B) Similar, with silver and gold iridescent abalones.

115—THREE VENETIAN GLASS VINAIGRETTES

Flat round and oval bodies; of light blue, deep sapphire-blue and rose-crimson, with aventurine grounds and silver-plated covers.

116—FOUR VENETIAN GLASS VINAIGRETTES

Three flat round and one oval; richly veined in varied blues, ivory and crimson, with gold grounds.

117—VIENNESE ENAMEL AND CRYSTAL FIGURINE

A gaily plumaged parrot; perched on a rustic tree-trunk supported on an oval crystal base enriched with enamels.

Height, 5 inches.

118—TWO ENAMELED SILVER GILT PATCH BOXES

By Tiffany, Paris

(A) Circular; with domed cover enriched in translucent red with blossom of a daisy.

(B) Similar, with brown ivory wreath and minute blue blossoms; on dull sky-blue ground.

119—DAINTY ENAMELED SILVER GILT BONBONNIÈRE

By Tiffany

Circular; with domed cover, enriched on translucent golden-yellow ground with numerous white blossomed green vine-lobes centered with blue dots, forming an intricate rosette.

120—ENAMELED SILVER GILDED BONBONNIÈRE   *By Tiffany*

Circular; with domed cover, enriched with golden-yellow blossom of a Black-eyed Susan.

121—ENAMEL GOLD PENDANT WATCH   *By Anton Werner*

Pear-shaped; in red enamel, with scalloped lace band at crown. Fine gold chain for suspension.

122—VIENNESE ENAMELED GOLD PENDANT WATCH

Louis Philippe Period

Cusped pear-shape; in red, arabesqued in gold and green. Fine gold chain for suspension.

123—VIENNESE ENAMEL VINAIGRETTE *Louis Philippe Period*

Bacchus' barrel, enriched with cupidons, vines of grapes and surmounting squirrel.

124—LAPIS-LAZULI AND ENAMELED GOLD DOUBLE CASE WATCH
English Eighteenth Century

Interior case, finely pierced and engraved with cupidons and daintily scrolled arabesques. Outer case of mother-of-pearl richly medallioned with lapis-lazuli and fine enamel scrollings. By Gabrier.

125—TWO PAIR OF ENAMELED GOLD SNAKE CHAIN BRACELETS

(A) Broad flat band, latticed with small round beads; finished with circular medallioned catch; enameled in black with vine leaves.

(B) Broader flat band, striped; finished with slide and fringed flat stop; enameled in black with varied key bandings.

126—TWO ETRUSCAN GOLD BROOCHES

Circular, open medallioned and spiraled cart-wheels.

127—JAPANESE GOLD BUTTON

Circular, of fine gold; enriched in low relief with quaint half-length figure of a "Japanese Juggler." Extremely fine modeling. Signed.

128—GOLD BEAD BRACELET

Flexible broad band of one hundred and thirty-five half-beads. Catch engraved with name and date.

129—TWO GOLD FILIGREE NECKLACES

(A) With trifoliated linked hexagon medallions.

(B) With varied cartouche-shaped medallions.

Lengths, 14 inches.

130—GOLD BEAD NECKLACE

Slightly graduated round beads. Engraved with initials.

Length, 16¼ inches.

131.—JEWELED GILDED BUCKLE   *Chinese, Ch'ien-lung Period*
Cabochon jade, tourmaline and carnelian. In gilded bronze leaf-scrolled settings.

132—JEWELED GILDED BUCKLE   *Chinese, Ch'ien-lung Period*
Cabochon carnelian, moss-agate and jade. In gilded bronze floral settings.

133.—GOLD FILIGREE LORGNETTE CHAIN
Dainty ovals of filigree; linked with small oval stops.
Length, **47** *inches.*

134—LONG GOLD LORGNETTE CHAIN
Round burnished beads; finished with triangular, engraved snap.
Length, **65** *inches.*

135—ENAMELED GOLD NECKLACE   *Louis Philippe Period*
Flexible striped oblong links; flanked by curved oblong medallions, enriched with blue arcades and floral motives on black. Extra snap at center to form two bracelets.
Length, **13¼** *inches.*

136—JEWELED GOLD NECKLACE   *East Indian*
Barbaric pendant, of three oval filigreed medallions. Surmounted by stellate motives, richly set with rubies, emeralds and pearls and fringed with many round beads. Slender oval and cruciform motived chain.
Length, **15** *inches.*

137—GOLD PENDENTED ABALONE NECKLACE
Two open pendants of floral motives in the "Noveau Art" manner; set with green and purple abalones. Slender oval link chain. 14-karat.
Length, **14¼** *inches.*

138—FILIGREE GOLD AND ABALONE NECKLACE
Oval medallions, set with green and pink iridescent abalones interrupted by open filigreed ovals of gold.
Length, **14** *inches.*

139—CARNELIAN AND GLASS NECKLACE
Egyptian, Second Century B.C.

Soft red carnelian vase-shaped pendent beads, alternating with similar motived semi-transparent glass beads; stopped with small round carnelians of similar color to those of vase shape. Centered with a stellated circular gold medallion.

Length, 16¾ inches.

140—CARNELIAN AND FAIENCE NECKLACE
Egyptian, Second Century B.C.

Composed of irregular round rich old-red carnelian stop-beads bearing at intervals curious turquoise-blue faience animalistic motived beads.

Length, 17¼ inches.

141—EARLY VENETIAN GLASS NECKLACE *Eighteenth Century*

Composed of faceted beads at front and hexagonal lozenge beads to neck; stopped by varied small gold and silver beads. Rare rich iridescent beads emulating the colors of most brilliant gems.

Length, 35 inches.

142—SAPPHIRE JEWELED GOLD LORGNETTE CHAIN

Faceted round sapphires of fancy hues, set in gold with very small links. Exceptionally brilliant delicately colored stones.

Length, 50 inches.

143—ROSETTED GOLD LORGNETTE CHAIN *East Indian*

Small round flat links, delicately rosetted in an alternate manner so as to be a continued string of dainty floral rosettes.

Length, 62½ inches.

144—JEWELED LOUIS XVI PENDANT

Composed of two red enameled graduated baskets of flowers suspended by vines of similar flowers to a gold snap. Silver gilded, set in the flowers with rose diamonds, sapphires, rubies and emeralds.

145—THREE JEWELED GOLD STUDS AND LINKS   *By Tiffany*

Lobed circular, stellate pierced fronts, daintily set with very brilliant rubies, emeralds, sapphires and rose diamonds. Three studs and two cuffs links.

146—SIX JEWELED SCARF PINS

Two enameled with floral motives; oval cabochon garnet, dog's head; heart with pearls; lavender enamel with seed pearls.

147—PEARL, TURQUOISE AND DIAMOND GOLD BAR PIN

Enriched with pearl stellate head, three oblongs of turquoise and central oblong set with old mine diamonds.

148—DIAMOND AND PEARL GOLD BAR PIN

Pin with Oriental pearl at crown and bee of open silver jeweled with rose diamonds.

149—BLACK PEARL JEWELED ENAMELED GOLD BAR PIN

Gold enameled black, everlasting knot. Set with lustrous Oriental black pearl.

150—PEARL SET GOLD MINIATURE LOCKET

Louis XVI Period

Oval, with porcelain head of a "Court Beauty," enriched, in gray hair, at ears and throat with rose diamonds. Surrounded by a setting of half pearls.

151—GOLD AND CARVED STONE SEAL

Seal cut in the form of an archaic shell. Gold swivel and mounting on black ribbon.

152—FOUR GOLD STUDS

Ball head, enriched with surrounding rope motive.

153—JEWELED SAPPHIRE AND MOONSTONE CUFF LINKS AND STUDS

Oval scrolled gold links, set with sapphires. Four similar links set with moonstones.

154—GOLD MESH HAIR NET

Finely latticed with squares; bordered with round gold beads.

5½ inches square.

155—GILDED STEEL BEADWORK COLLAR

Three oblong panels, worked with arabesque of steel and rose beads; connected by numerous strands of single gilded beads.

156—FINE GOLD MESH OPERA BAG

Diamond lattice chain; with Vandyke crown, trimmed with gadrooned beads. Snake chain double pull set in twisted round links.

·Depth, 8¼ inches.

157—FINE GOLD MESH PURSE

Long eighteenth century stocking shape; scale linked. Rounded ends set with rose diamonds in silver.

Length, 24½ inches.

158—JEWELED BEADED BAG

Spade shape; worked in fine varicolored beads with rose garlanded lyres. Silver-gilded clasp enriched with cupidons and scrollings, set with abalones and semi-precious stones. Link chain for suspension.

Width, 7½ inches; depth, 9½ inches.

159—JEWELED GOLD MESH BAG

Wrought in 14-karat gold. Oblong plain frame, with cabochon sapphire catch. Chain mail mesh; oblong link chain handle.

Length, 6 inches.

160—HINDU-PERSE FAN AND LACQUER CASE

Eighteenth Century

Pierced light even yellow tortoise-shell fan; enriched with medallions, pinnacles, scrollings and panel of pagoda-like building.

Lacquer Pen Case, Persian; decorated with medallions of beautiful flowers.

Length, 8¾ inches.

161—JEWELED PEARL GOLD PEN

Fluted tapering pen, set at head with a lustrous Oriental pearl. In red leather case.

Length, 8 inches.

162—FORTY ORIENTAL PEARLS

Fine round pearls; varying in color and lustre.

163—TWO AMETHYST JEWELED GOLD CUFF STUDS

Large faceted brilliant amethysts; open settings with beaded edges.

164—DIAMOND AND PEARL BROOCH

Large lustrous Oriental central pearl; set with diamond motive of old mine stones and four smaller outer pearls.

165—DIAMOND AND PEARL BROOCH

Five-starred circular brooch, set with twelve finely graduated Oriental pearls and intervening stellate of rose diamonds.

166—JEWELED EMERALD AND ROSE DIAMOND BAR PIN

Gold pin, finished with a rosette of rose diamonds; supporting open monogram E.M. in rose diamonds and emeralds. (Several chips missing.)

167—JEWELED AMERICAN FLAG

Gold, finely jeweled with innumerable rubies, diamonds and sapphires.

168—DIAMOND RUBY AND EMERALD BUCKLE   *East Indian*

Circular gold, set with inner cabochon and outer series of lobed rubies; interrupted by emeralds and diamonds. Enameled back.

169—JEWELED TRANSLUCENT ENAMEL BROOCH   *By Gaillard*

Oval, with open golden-green ivy leaves, surrounded by clusters of Oriental seed pearls. Oblong faceted topaz at center.

170—Two Japanese Cultured Pearl Scarf Pins

Pink and silvery iridescence. Mounted in open aster silver setting.

171—Two Japanese Cultured Pearl Scarf Pins

Similar to the preceding.

172—Pearl and Diamond Pin

Gold pin, set with diamond at head and lustrous Oriental pearl drop.

173—Culture Japanese Pearl Bar Pin

Triangular gold bar, set with lustrous round pearl.

174—Two Pearl Bar Pins

Seven cultured Japanese pearls of fine lustre, closely set on a gold bar.

175—Japanese Cultured Pearl Bar Pin

Nine lustrous silvery pearls; set on a medallioned gold bar.

176—Japanese Cultured Pearl Bar Pin

Three graduated lustrous pearls; set on a diamond motived gold bar.

177—Japanese Cultured Pearl Brooch

Sixteen lustrous silvery pearls, set in an annular gold ring.

178—Four Coral Studs and Two Links

Finely matched round pink corals; clasp set with small rose diamonds.

179—Diamond Neckband Slide

Open arched oblong of gold; set with brilliant old mine diamonds. On black velvet band.

180—Jeweled Translucent Enamel Hair-comb *By Lalique*

Arched gold oblong; enriched with lavender lotus flower sprays amid a platinum water motive, adorned with diamonds. Hinged tortoise-shell comb at back.

181—EAST INDIAN PEARL BROOCH

Circular gold brooch, set with thirty-two deep lustred Oriental pearls.

182—EAST INDIAN PEARL BROOCH

Similar to the preceding.

183—PLAQUETTE OF ORIENTAL PEARLS

Square, with gold-embroidered ground enriched with about two hundred Oriental seed pearls.

184—TWO LUSTROUS BLACK PEARL EARRINGS

Shimmering gun metal Oriental pearls; set in diamond enriched gold safety clasps. Pearls about twenty grains each.

(*Illustrated*)

185—DIAMOND AND PLATINUM NECK CHAIN

Bowknot with laurel-leaf festoons and small chained clasp. Enriched with rose diamonds and beautiful pendant set with old mine diamond. Mounted on black velvet band. Pendant diamond approximately 2½ karats. Made by Boucheron, Paris.

(*Illustrated*)

186—BEAUTIFUL DIAMOND PLATINUM COLLAR

Composed of sixteen interlacing and entwining platinum bowknots, gracefully arranged and closely set with innumerable diamonds. Charming circular six-stone clasp in gold.

(*Illustrated*)   *Length, 13½ inches.*

187—IMPORTANT PEARL AND DIAMOND DOG COLLAR

By Tiffany

Composed of ten strands, of well matched lustrous Oriental pearls numbering nine hundred and ninety. Interrupted by five vertical bars of platinum set with diamonds numbering forty-five.   *Length, 13⅛ inches.*

(*Illustrated*)

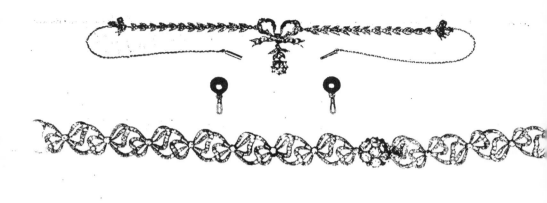

No. 185—Diamond and Platinum Neck Chain
No. 184—Two Lustrous Black Pearl Earrings
No. 186—Beautiful Diamond Platinum Collar
No. 187—Important Pearl and Diamond Dog Collar

188—OLD MINE DIAMOND BROOCH AND EARRINGS

Crescent brooch, with two tapering pendent drops, of gold, set closely with very brilliant old mine stones (one drop, central star and three diamonds are loose). Crescent earrings, with beautiful large drop diamond and similar single tapering pendant. Two large diamonds, 5 karats.

189—DIAMOND BROOCH

Open scrolled gold setting bearing center and seven surrounding diamonds. Fitted with small ring as a pendant. Eight diamonds; approximate weight, 1.50 karats.

190—ORIENTAL SEED PEARL COLLAR AND CHAIN

Collar, basketed with diamond motives; silver clasp chain, with four perfect strands only in place; but two packages of sufficient pearls accompany chain to complete strands. Mounted in silver, with diamond-studded domes and large pearls supporting many fringe tassels.

> Collar: Length, 13¼ inches.
> Chain: Length, 28½ inches.

191—GOLD LORGNETTE CHAIN

Set with seventy-three Oriental sapphires. (Imperfect.)

192—DIAMOND AND SAPPHIRE BEE BROOCH

In the form of a bee; closely set in gold with two cabochon sapphires and forty-six diamonds. Diamonds approximately 4½ karats.

193—VERY IMPORTANT DIAMOND SUNBURST

Similar to the preceding. Center stone 2.25 karats; the remaining stones approximately 35 karats.

194—DIAMOND CRESCENT BAR PIN

Gold and silver, closely set with varied old mine stones. Composed of one hundred and sixteen graduated diamonds. Approximately 18 karats.

195—BROKEN ORIENTAL BAROQUE PEARL COLLAR

Composed of one thousand small pearls varying in quality.

196—Nine Varied Emeralds

Two cabochons, seven faceted oblong stones. 17.35 karats.

197—Fine Diamond Sunburst

Circular center, with surrounding whorls of diamonds; closely set in silver and gold with old mine stones, carefully graduated. Center stone of 1.40 karats; fifty surrounding stones, approximately 5½ karats. Not including the many rose diamonds at points.

198—Fine Diamond Sunburst

Similar to the preceding.

199—Important Diamond Sunburst

Similar to the preceding; larger. Center stone 2.25 karats; seventy-two surrounding stones approximately 8.75 karats.

200—Jet and Gold Beadwork Bag

Blunt shade shape. Enriched with gold and black diamond motives, the gold predominating alternately; studded with faceted jet centers; Vandyke fringe. Oblong gun-metal frame set with faceted oblongs of jet chain handle.

Depth, 8 inches; width, 6⅜ inches.

201—Sardonyx and Sapphire Parasol Handle and Tips

By Tiffany

Open stellated leaf-motived globular handle and ferrule in lemon gold, richly set with large sardonyx and smaller sapphires. Tips and rings to match. In leather case.

202—East Indian Jewel Gold and Crystal Perfume Bottle

Flat oval crystal bottle (has been repaired at neck, but unseen). Mounted with gold neck and hinged dome cover, spirally enameled in emerald green; studded with rubies, diamonds and pearl terminal. (Two stones missing.)

RUSSIAN SABLE, BROADTAIL, SEALSKIN AND OTHER FURS

203—Two Rare Lemur Pelts

Remarkably marked gray pelts.

Length, 21 inches; width, 18 inches.

204—Badger Foot-warmer

Spade shape; edged with leopard skin. Lined with white Astrachan. (Leather cover slightly rubbed.)

Length, 14 inches.

205—Small Caracal Scarf

Lustrous pelt, with flaring lobed ends. Lined black satin.

Length, 34 inches.

206—Gray Krimmer

Natural-shaped pelt; interestingly marked.

Length, 22 inches; width, 25 inches.

207—Natural Seal Pillow Muff

Beautifully marked with golden tones at corners. Lined with fawn satin.

Length, 13½ inches.

208—Natural Raccoon Pillow Muff

Long-haired finely marked pelt; lined with wallaby.

Length, 14½ inches.

209—Scotch Mole Tie Scarf and Canteen Muff

Rich lustrous pelts. Lined with plum-gray satin.

Scarf: Length, 32½ inches.

Muff: Length, 12 inches.

210—NATURAL MONKEY MUFF

Round; richly flecked with golden tones. Lined with brown satin.

Length, 10½ inches.

211—CHINCHILLA PLATEAU

Hat crown; circular. Five well-matched pelts.

Diameter, 13½ inches.

212—BROADTAIL CANTEEN MUFF

Very beautifully marked rich pelts. Lined with black satin.

Length, 12½ inches.

213—BLACK FOX STOLE

Long-haired rich pelt, finished with two claws and long tails at each end. Lined with black satin. Two pelts.

Length, 69 inches.

214—BROADTAIL SMALL MUFF AND COLLAR

Pillow muff; mounted with head at crown and black ribbon bow. Shaped collar unfinished.

Muff: Length, 8½ inches.

Collar: Length, 47 inches.

215—UNPLUCKED OTTER MUFF

Pillow shape; rich brown pelt, with tortoise-shell ring handle. Lined with ivory satin.

Length, 15 inches.

216—LENGTH OF UNPLUCKED OTTER

Rich close fur of beautiful even quality. Suitable for collar, revers or cuffs, for a man's coat.

Length, 2 yards 19 inches; width, 7½ inches.

217—SILVER FOX ANIMAL SCARF

Long-furred pelt, finely marked with silver. Head and paws mounted. (Slightly rubbed at sides.)

Length, 52 inches.

218—Small Russian Sable Choker Scarf

Shaped scarf; well matched. Lined with ivory satin. Two skins.

Length, 32 inches.

219—Russian Sable Pillow Muff

Lustrous richly marked pelts; finished with eight tails at foot. Lined with brown satin. Four pelts.

Length, 15 inches; depth, 19 inches.

220—Russian Sable Small Boa

Richly marked pelt; finished at ends with claws and three tails, at center of back with group of five tails. Two skins; slightly rubbed at sides.

Length, 48 inches.

221—Silver Fox Animal Scarf

Beautiful long-furred pelt, finely marked. Head mounted.

Length, 57 inches.

222—Russian Sable Boa

Rich brown pelt, mounted with three tails at each end and four groups of two at four intervals. Five pelts of Kamtchatka origin.

Length, 2 yards 15 inches.

223—Natural Seal Coat

Rich close pelts, well matched. High collar and deep revers. Lined with ivory bird patterned silk. (Edges slightly rubbed.)

Length, 48 inches.

224—Mink Cape

Rich, finely matched pelts; with small collar. Lined with golden-yellow. Forty-five pelts.

Length, 27 inches; width, 66 inches.

225—Hudson Bay Sable Coat

Lustrous; finely matched and marked pelts. Deep collar, revers and cuffs. Lined with floral yellow silk damask. About seventy-five pelts. A most distinguished piece of fur apparel.

Length, 52 inches.

(Illustrated—See also Frontispiece)

No. 225—Hudson Bay Sable Coat

226—LADY'S BLACK BABY CARACAL COAT

Very lustrous finely marked pelt; small collar. Trimmed with broad and narrow soutache braid. Lined with fawn satin. (Rubbed on sides and edges; slight tears.)

Length, 40 *inches.*

227—ALASKAN SEAL COAT

Rich deep-toned pelts; trimmed with lighter toned sea-otter high collar and cuffs. Seal belt for same. Lined with gray floral silk.

Length, 39 *inches.*

228—BROADTAIL COAT

Beautifully matched pelts; with deep collar and cuffs. Long loose belt. Lined with floral rose-du-Barry silk.

Length, 41 *inches.*

AMERICAN ART ASSOCIATION,

MANAGERS.

THOMAS E. KIRBY,

AUCTIONEER.

SD - #0161 - 121222 - C0 - 229/152/3 - PB - 9780266261919 - Gloss Lamination